The Arab World
Tents to City Sidewalks

Tents to City Sidewalks
by Doreen Ingrams

Photography by
Alistair Duncan,
Anthony Howarth
and others

EMC Corporation
St. Paul, Minnesota

Library of Congress Cataloging in Publication Data

Ingrams, Doreen.
  Tents to city sidewalks.

  (Her The Arab world)
  SUMMARY: Photographs and brief text contrast the nomadic, village, and city life styles
of the Arab people.
    1. Arab countries—Social life and customs—Juvenile literature. [1. Arab countries—Social
life and customs] I. Duncan, Alistair, 1927–   illus. II. Howarth, Anthony, illus. III. Title.
DS36.78.I54   910'.09'174927   74-16154
ISBN 0-88436-113-6

Published by EMC Corporation
180 East Sixth Street
St. Paul, Minnesota 55101
Printed in the United States of America
0 9 8 7 6 5 4 3 2

The Arab World
Tents to City Sidewalks
New Ways for Ancient Lands
Mosques and Minarets

Introducing the Arabs

What is an Arab? To most of us, the word brings pictures of the desert. In fact, that is what "Arab" really means — "a man of the desert." The Arab people first came from the deserts of the Arabian Peninsula. During the seventh century they spread out and took over countries to the north, east, and west of them. Today, after thirteen hundred years, the Arab World reaches from Morocco on the Atlantic Ocean to Iraq and the small states of the Arabian Gulf.

The Arab World lies on two continents — Africa and Asia. It consists of nineteen separate countries with varying social, economic, and political conditions. Its people number 135 million.

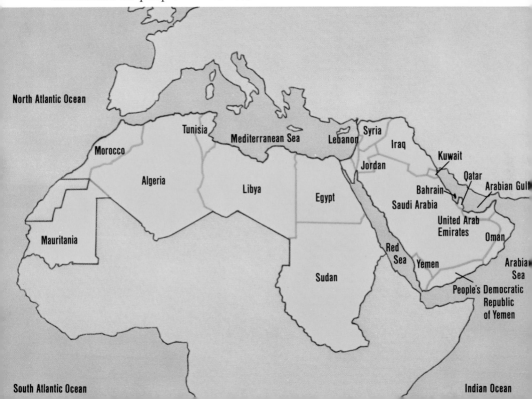

A nomad caravan in Judea, west of the river Jordan. Even today, these desert people live much the same way as their ancestors did many centuries ago.

Across this broad region of North Africa and the Middle East, there are many separate countries. But the people of the Arab nations are united by two strong ties — language and religion. They all speak Arabic and nearly all of them, ninety percent, follow one of the world's major religions, Islam.

Although they speak the same language and most share the same religious beliefs, you would find there are differences between the people of one Arab country and another. They may speak a different dialect or wear a special kind of clothing. You can often tell where people come from just by their style of dress or by listening to them speak.

There are also economic and social differences between Arab countries. Today some are modern, prosperous states, with huge incomes from oil. Others have no natural resources to bring in money. These are poor and undeveloped. But no matter which country you visit, you will find three distinct life styles — that of the nomad, the villager, and the city dweller.

A typical village market scene in Egypt. Most villagers in inland areas are farmers, raising field crops or fruit like the oranges shown here. In many parts of the Arab World only men go to the market.

Algiers, capital city of Algeria in North Africa, offers many contrasts. On a typical downtown street men and women in Western-style clothing walk side by side with others in traditional Arab dress. The woman in the center veils the lower part of her face in the age-old fashion and is completely covered from head to foot.

Desert Wanderers

The desert, a vast and lonely expanse of sand and barren stone, is a harsh reality in much of the Arab World. There is little rain in Arab lands and much of the soil is too poor to farm. Since early times, the Arabs have learned to live in a hostile environment. Many have lived as herdsmen, traveling from place to place looking for water and grass for their animals. These wandering people, the Bedouin nomads, now represent only four to five percent of the total Arab population. But they have a rich heritage that has survived over many centuries.

The homes of the Bedouin nomads are very simple. But these tents made of goats' hair offer shelter from the wind, shade from the sun, and protection from rain.

The wandering desert life has been the way of the Bedouin for centuries and he does not wish to change it, even today. Modern Arab governments are encouraging the nomads to settle in fertile village areas or to take jobs in the new city industries. But the Bedouin resists, clinging to his age-old life style.

This Bedouin rides on a saddle that has large, hanging saddlebags with tassels. He does not use reins. Instead he holds a rope which may be attached to a halter or pulled through a hole in the camel's nose. When the rider wants to change direction, he simply gives the rope a pull. When he wants the camel to halt, he pulls its head up as the man does here.

A camel has a very smug and pompous expression. The Bedouin say this is because, although Arabs know ninety-nine different names for God, the camel knows the hundredth.

These nomadic people belong to different tribes and each tribe has its own territory which may cover hundreds of miles. All of the members of a Bedouin's tribe will be related to him by blood or through marriage. If his tribe is a large one with many members, it will be divided into clans. Each clan will be divided again into sections, and each section will be made up of a group of families. Each clan, section, and family has its own chief. He is responsible for settling disputes and for advising his people and making decisions for his own group. The leading tribal chief is selected from among these lesser chiefs of the tribe.

The Bedouin have names very different from those we are used to. When a child is born into a tribal family, it is given a name such as Ali, if he is a boy, or Ayesha, if she is a girl. There are no last names in Arab culture, so the father's name is used to help identify people. The boy may be called Ali bin (son of) Muhammad, or the girl may be known as Ayesha bint (daughter of) Muhammad. But there will be many other people with these same names, so the name of the clan or tribe is also added. A boy's full name might be Ali bin Muhammad al Amiri. That is, "Ali the son of Muhammad of the Amiri tribe." A girl might have the full name of Ayesha bint Muhammad al Hamumi, meaning "Ayesha the daughter of Muhammad of the Hamumi tribe."

Most Bedouin make their living by raising camels, goats, and sheep. The members of the group travel in caravans from one grazing area to another. If there has been rain, they know where to find water in the desert. In dry months, they move closer to farming areas where they can find streams, springs, or wells.

Since the Bedouin are constantly on the move, they have no permanent houses. In most desert areas they live in tents made of goats' hair. The hair is spun into thread, then woven into long pieces of cloth which can be fixed to wooden poles. The tents are quite large and are divided by curtains to provide separate quarters for men and women. But they are easily taken down and loaded onto camels when it is time to move on to another place.

Camels do not usually stray far from the tents. But if they do get lost, the Bedouin are very clever at following their tracks. Bedouin are also noted for their ability to find their way in deserts and to use the stars as direction-finders.

These camels are waiting to have loads tied onto the wooden frames that have been laid across their humps. A camel is always made to sit while being loaded.

Donkeys are more surefooted than camels and so are better for riding over stony mountain passes. But a donkey cannot go for long without water or food. A camel can survive for days without food and for even longer periods without water.

Waterholes in the desert are often the only source of drink for the animals. When the water left by rain in the waterhole has evaporated or been used up, the nomads have to move on to other sources of water.

14

In southern Arabia, Bedouin families have no tents. Instead they sleep in caves on the sides of dry river beds or take shelter under the scant shade of a thorn tree. Sometimes, when they find a source of water, they will build huts of palm branches and become partially settled. I traveled hundreds of miles with Bedouin and often we would pass a group of abandoned huts left by a group that had moved on after the nearby water pool had dried up.

Moving day is a simple matter for a Bedouin family. They have only the few possessions they can carry with them — lamps, water pots, cooking and eating utensils. Today, perhaps, a nomad family might also own a sewing machine and a transistor radio. Their food supply will include dates, coffee, flour, and sometimes dried fish and spices. The goats and sheep provide meat and wool, and from the goats and camels they get milk and cheese. Bread, made from millet or wheat flour, is fried or roasted in the embers of a fire rather than being baked. Sometimes, as a treat, rice is bought at village markets. If the caravan comes across a gazelle or other wild game, the Bedouin will shoot it for extra meat.

In some parts of the Arab World, looking after goats and sheep is a man's duty. In others, only the women and girls herd the flocks. Herding is hard work. It often means walking many miles to find enough grazing for the animals.

For all his free, wandering life, a Bedouin still needs money for some necessities and comforts — flour for bread, kerosene and matches for the lamps, a new cooking utensil, or cloth for the family's clothing. To get these, he may sell some of his animals in a village market. Or he may be hired by a town merchant to carry goods by camel or donkey to a remote settlement along his caravan route. But today, as more roads wind through the desert, trucks are beginning to replace the camel caravans of the nomads. This means that an important source of needed income for the nomads is disappearing. Some day this may force them to settle in villages and give up their nomadic way of life.

Boys and girls begin to help with the family duties at an early age. Bedouin boys work with their fathers, taking care of the camels or helping with the loads. Boys of six can be seen leading a string of camels as they plod all day through the desert heat. If a boy gets tired, he will scramble up one side of a moving camel and perch crosslegged on top of its load until he feels rested. As soon as a Bedouin boy earns enough money for himself, he will buy a curved dagger to wear in his belt. This will be his proudest possession, for all Bedouin men wear them.

A girl, too, will have important responsibilities. She learns to fetch water, gather firewood, herd goats or sheep, cook, spin, weave, and sew her own clothes. Like the boys, the girls learn to become self-reliant at an early age. I have met little girls, all alone and far away from the rest of the group, watching over their goats. With them they have only a handful of dates to eat from early morning until they return to the tents at sunset.

For centuries, Bedouin boys and girls never went to school or saw a doctor. Today, when a tribe is camped near a town, the children can go to school and there will be medical treatment available for members of the tribe who need it. But even if the children never attend school, their parents will teach them about their religion — Islam. All must learn to say their prayers and to recite passages by heart from their holy book, the Koran.

While the men are away with the camels, Bedouin women sometimes have to walk long distances to fetch water. Today, tins and plastic buckets are replacing the traditional and beautiful earthenware jars as water-carriers.

These nomad women from Oman are veiled. But many Bedouin women do not wear veils and are much freer than Arab women living in villages or towns.

The Bedouin are fond of music and stories. Often the men bring out a reed pipe and play melancholy tunes to while away the time while traveling or sitting around the campfire at night after a long day's ride. I have listened to them exchanging old tales of their tribal history — the bravery of fathers in battle long ago, or other tribal legends that have been passed on from fathers to sons and mothers to daughters over many generations. Reciting poetry is another favorite evening pastime. But today, the transistor radio often replaces the story teller or singer around the campfire, bringing music from the far-off cities or news of the outside world. Almost every Bedouin family owns a transistor, a welcome voice in the desert night.

The Bedouin use no chairs, but they are quite happy sitting cross-legged on the ground. They will sit for hours listening to a storyteller or to someone bringing the latest news from the towns. Or perhaps they will listen to their transistor radios, tuning in to an Arab station or to Voice of America or British Arabic Service broadcasts.

The lonely, wandering way of life has made the Bedouin a hospitable people. They never let a traveler pass by without offering him food and coffee or tea. When I traveled I always took coffee beans with me and, on arriving at a Bedouin camp, I would offer a handful to my host. He, in turn, would roast the beans and hand them around on a homemade, braided straw plate so that we could all enjoy the rich aroma. Then he would add them to the coffee pot brewing over the wood fire.

A guest will sometimes stay at a Bedouin camp for two to three days but, out of courtesy to your hosts, you never stay *more* than three days. Gifts are always exchanged when leaving.

Perhaps, if you compared the Bedouin life to your own, you might think it simple and hard. But the nomads accept it as the will of God. In their own eyes they are the "true" Arabs, stronger and better than the soft-living people of the villages and cities. And they are fiercely proud of their desert tradition.

But as the Arab World moves into a more modern industrial society, many of these proud desert wanderers are being absorbed into a different way of life. They are moving into towns or settling on the land. Some day, there may be no more nomad caravans crossing the old tribal lands. But we can hope that the Bedouin tradition of endurance, hospitality, and simple honesty will not disappear.

The Villagers

There is a picturesque air about an Arab village. It may lie along the banks of a river in Egypt or perhaps it perches precariously atop a mountain in Yemen. The colors of the local stone or mud brick houses blend in with the sand-colored landscape, broken only by the green of the date palms and the cultivated fields and orchards of the Arab farmers.

Arab villagers build their homes of materials close at hand. Sometimes they are made of stone, but more often they are made of rectangular-shaped bricks made of mud mixed with straw and dried hard in the sun. To keep the mud from dissolving in heavy rain, the roofs of the mud-brick houses are protected with a whitewash coating.

Usually the Arab houses are only one or two stories high. But in Yemen and southern Arabia, particularly in the region called Hadhramaut, the houses may be as high as seven stories. They have been called "the skyscrapers of the desert," and indeed they are very high for houses made of mud on a foundation of stone. These houses have a central pillar with a staircase around it. Each story is a few inches narrower than the one below, giving the building a slightly tapered look. The roofs are flat and have gutters attached to them so that when it rains, the water can run safely down into the street.

Glass is still hard to get in many remote Arab villages and the houses often have wooden shutters on the windows to keep out the sun and the cold. High in the mountain villages of Yemen the Arabs use alabaster for their windows. This soft white mineral is found in the nearby mountains and can be used like glass. It keeps out the cold and lets in a dim, golden light.

In the mountains of the Yemen Arab Republic, villages perch on the sides of steep cliffs. Unlike village dwellings in much of the Arab World, the houses here are several stories high.

The minaret of the village mosque stands high among the village houses just as the steeple of the village church in other lands can be seen from afar. At one time the mosque had the only school available in the village. Arab boys would go to the mosque school to learn the Koran and perhaps simple arithmetic. But girls were not allowed to go to school at all. Now the Arab countries are building schools and training teachers. Today, most Arab children, even in remote villages, are able to go to school.

A village usually began when a wandering tribe decided to settle in one place and farm the land. The chief of the tribe usually became the head of the village and it was his job to give advice and settle the disputes.

Today the villages have more contact with the central governments and get more services for their people. Many have electricity and running water which they never had before. And some have clinics or visiting doctors to treat the sick. Not very many years ago a villager who became sick was treated with herbal remedies or even branded with a hot iron. Charms were used to ward off evil spirits.

This village in Saudi Arabia is built above the level of the flood water. When the water rushes down the valley after a heavy rain it irrigates the crops and trees.

These two Egyptian village women are wearing clothes made of cloth dyed with indigo. Many villagers and Bedouin like to wear dark-colored clothes.

The women are standing beside a pile of bricks which will be used for building a house.

But the villager, following his Muslim faith, accepts both pain and pleasure. "Praise be to God" he says, for either one.

Most of the Arab families in the villages are farmers. They work at cultivating plots of land in the valleys or wherever there is enough water. Even women and children may work in the fields, especially at harvest time. But home tasks keep them busy too. They carry water from the well or stream, bring in firewood, and herd goats and sheep. Many still spin and weave their own clothes.

In the courtyard of a village house in Iraq, the women have been busy washing the bedclothes. The girl in the background is taking bread from the oven.

The other picture shows a close-up of the oven which is built of clay. It is preheated with firewood. When the fire has died down, the bread dough is rolled out flat and slapped against the sides of the oven. It sticks there and bakes in the heat of the oven wall. In three to five minutes, the flat bread is ready to be peeled off for eating.

Irrigation is very difficult for the Arab farmer, for there are very few rivers in the Arab countries. Farmers must depend on rainfall for their water supply and it seldom rains. When it does, they try to dam the floodwaters. But much of it flows into the sea or the desert sands and is lost for the crops. The pools that sometimes form after a heavy rain quickly evaporate or are used up in a few weeks.

Water left behind by the floods after a heavy rain brings these Saudi Arabian villagers out to enjoy the scene. When it rains the children run out into the roads to splash and bathe in the puddles.

I was once caught in one of the flash floods that frequently follow a heavy rain. It had been raining steadily for several hours. In a few moments the dry river bed in the valley became a raging torrent carrying everything before it. Trees were uprooted and any sheep and goats that were in its path were drowned.

In the highlands, the farmers have become very skillful at terrace cultivation. Terracing prevents soil erosion and makes the best possible use of rain water.

For a more permanent supply of water, some farmers have dug deep wells. Sometimes the well has a mechanical pump. But often the water is still drawn, as it has been for ages, by a team of animals. The creaking of the pulley, the cries of the animals, and the chanting, rhythmic songs of the men as the water is brought up blend into a haunting sound.

Village women use all sorts of containers to fetch water, from plastic buckets to aluminum saucepans to earthenware jars. Running water in the house is rare in places outside the cities.

At harvest time all the family help in the fields. The donkey looks heavy-laden, but since the load is only straw, it is really quite light.

The streets of the village are usually narrow alleys. The open spaces are unpaved and littered with trash and garbage. Dogs, cats, and hens scavenge for scraps of food, scrambling and dodging the hooves of the camels and donkeys, the carts, and the people who crowd the streets. Flies are everywhere.

In most villages there is at least one "general" shop, where villagers and Bedouin can buy the necessities they can't glean from the land, such as kerosene, matches, tools, and groceries such as salt, tea, and rice.

And there are village craftsmen. Potters sell their earthenware jars and bowls. Tinsmiths make pans for cooking. Silversmiths create jewelry and ornaments — earrings, bracelets, necklaces, and rings. A village scribe writes letters for those who cannot read or write.

The larger villages have weekly market days, usually named for the day it is held — such as Wednesday market or Thursday market. Villagers and Bedouin come from miles around, their camels and donkeys laden with farm products or crafts for the local shops. They bring vegetables, eggs, chickens, goats and sheep, woven mats, earthenware pots, and many other goods.

The narrow streets are filled with noisy bargaining, vendors calling out their wares, drivers who call out continuously to warn other marketers out of the way of their carts and camels. On market day the villagers have a chance to gossip and exchange news, so it becomes a social occasion as well as a shopping and selling excursion.

There are few such diversions in the life of the villagers, except for an occasional wedding or holy day. Then the men gather in one place and the women in another to dance, sing, and feast.

This village in Iraq has a whole street of small shops. It also has a coffee shop where the men can sit and gossip.

Two horsetraders exchange traditional greetings before bargaining at a village market in Oman. Touching noses is a custom only in certain parts of the Arab World. It is more common to shake hands or kiss on both cheeks.

Villagers and Bedouin come from many miles around to this weekly market in Oman. They bring animals or produce such as grain, eggs, or cheese to sell. Then they are able to buy cloth, ornaments, and fodder for their animals.

More and more villagers can now bring their produce to market by truck, rather than by camel or donkey.

Weaving is a typical village industry. Sometimes the women join together to make carpets or colorful and beautifully patterned pieces of woven cloth.

A village silversmith does a good business. In the past there were no banks in villages for depositing savings, so villagers bought gold or silver ornaments which could be resold if money was needed. Such ornaments are still popular today.

Most of the time the villagers go to bed early and rise early. As dawn breaks, the *muezzin* — the man who calls the people to prayer from the minaret of the village mosque — urges villagers to rise and say their prayers. "Prayers are better than sleep," he cries.

Soon, the smoke rising from the rooftops shows that the women are preparing the breakfast of coffee, bread and honey, or goat cheese. Then there is a stir as the men lead the oxen or donkeys out to the fields and the women go to fetch water.

The Arab village homes are usually furnished simply with carpets or woven mats. Everyone takes off his shoes at the door so the dirt of the streets is not tracked onto the carpets. The women's rooms are separate from the men's. They are called the *harem*, which means "forbidden."

Not all the Arab communities have such hard and fast rules about separation of the sexes, but in general it is the custom for village men and women to keep themselves apart. I have stayed in a village home where I was quickly surrounded by the women of the house and their friends. Many of them had never seen a European before. But when the men wanted to come and talk, the women all disappeared.

It is a great treat to visit an Arab village home. Remember to take off your shoes at the door. First you shake hands with your host and anyone else present. Then you sit down on the floor crosslegged, or "tailor fashion," with your legs tucked under you as you lean against the cushions along the wall.

Coffee or tea will most certainly be offered, and you will likely be invited to share the family meal. The Arabs are very hospitable people.

The main meal is eaten at midday. This is quite simple — bread, perhaps rice, boiled meat, or a dish of vegetables in a spicy sauce. Of course this menu will not be the same in every country of the Arab world.

Before you eat, a bowl, a towel, and a cake of soap will be brought for you to use to wash your hands. Then the meal will be spread out on a cloth or perhaps on a plaited straw tray.

Your host will begin the meal by saying quietly, "In the name of God." You are to eat with your right hand only and, like the villagers, you will eat with your fingers. When you have finished eating you wash again. After the midday meal the family rests during the heat of the early afternoon.

Later in the afternoon the men go back to the fields. They return home again at sunset. The village day is punctuated by calls to prayer at dawn, midday, mid-afternoon, sunset, and during the evening.

As daylight fades the women light the oil lamps and prepare the evening meal. Afterwards the men may go to the local coffee shop to gossip or to listen to the radio while they drink coffee and smoke a water-cooled pipe, or *hookah*, which they pass around from one to another. Meanwhile the women may visit each other's houses.

Later, but not very late, everyone returns home. Then the woven mats that serve as beds in many Arab homes will be unrolled and made ready for sleeping. Silence falls as the lights and lamps of the village go out one by one.

Villagers along the banks of the Nile and other rivers earn their living by fishing. Fresh water varieties include perch, catfish, mullet, and eels.

The Arab World has long coastlines and fishing is an important resource for village communities by the sea. The fishermen use nets or traps made of wickerwork. The most common fish caught are shark, tuna, bonito, mackerel, and sardines.

The City Dwellers

Cities of the world all resemble each other in some ways. The sound of traffic is the same in Cairo as it is in New York. Aircraft fly over most modern cities on their way to and from the airports. Music entices you into cafes or amusement parks whether in Beirut or Chicago. Yet, if you suddenly found yourself in an Arab city, you would be aware of the differences as well as the similarities between it and a city in the West.

A bird's-eye view of the seaport city of Tripoli in Lebanon, on the Mediterranean Sea. An ancient city, it is now also an important modern commercial center with a mainly Muslim population. Lebanon is unique in the Arab World because it has an almost equal number of Christians and Muslims.

In the oil-rich countries of Saudi Arabia and Kuwait, there are brand new cities built in the desert for people in brand new jobs created by the wealth that oil has produced. These cities have no past except that of the small tribal villages or Bedouin camps that once established their shallow roots there. But other cities like Cairo, Tunis. Baghdad, and Damascus have fabulous histories reaching far back in time — histories that can still be seen in their turreted forts, the domed shops, the ornate mosques and palaces.

In contrast to Tripoli, Dubai is a new oil-producing city which grew out of a small trading center on the Arabian Gulf. The city is divided in half by a creek, which can be seen at the upper left.

Old houses can still be found among the modern high-rises of Jeddah in Saudi Arabia. These were the homes of traders and government officials in the days when Jeddah was a little-known commercial port on the Red Sea. The shuttered balconies are part of the women's quarters. Screened by the shutters, the women of the house can look onto the street without being seen.

Beirut is a cosmopolitan city and its people have long been in touch with the Western world and Western ideas. This is reflected in the city's new architecture, like these high-rise apartments.

Just as there are contrasts of old and new Arab cities, so there are contrasts in life styles within the urban centers. Businessmen and government officials in well-tailored suits walk or drive to their offices. A man in traditional cotton robes persistently offers a tray full of picture postcards for sale, or shoe laces, combs, and other oddments. Small boys in long shirts clamor to clean the shoes of the tourists.

The pattern of life for Arab businessmen will be much the same as their counterparts in Chicago or Toronto. Their daily jobs demand regular business hours and a routine that fits the commercial schedule in other parts of the world. After breakfast the Arab executive leaves his house or apartment by auto. He heads to work in an air-conditioned office building. His wife does her shopping in a modern store and his children go off to school just like children in any city.

But men and boys who earn their living as street peddlers are apt to live in one of the shanty towns that ring almost every large Arab city. The children play in the streets, run errands for shopkeepers, or carry parcels for shoppers — earning a few pennies whenever, wherever they can.

A city worker in San'a, Yemen Arab Republic, tells his children to smile for the camera. The furnishings of this room are typical of a traditional Arab home. People sit on the floor, on rugs or carpets, with cushions at their backs. Modern touches here are the transistor radio and the pile of Western-style magazines at the right.

Some women walk briskly along in pants or short skirts, their hair fashionably styled. Others walk past at a leisurely pace wearing traditional black cloaks, their heads covered, their faces veiled.

Arab cities contain all that is modern and much that is steeped in culture of the ages. They are filled with people, but the typical city still does not have enough industry to keep them all gainfully employed. Most cities are still centers of trade with little or no manufacturing. Therefore, jobs are provided for the smallest and simplest tasks. Every building has an abundance of messengers, doorkeepers, men to find places for cars to park. Many of these people, in turn, have helpers. Since the cost of labor is cheap, the businesses of the city employ many people and divide each job into assorted small jobs. Thus, everyone has a little money to live on.

Between the rich-and-powerful and the poor-and-struggling is a vital and growing force in the Arab world — the new middle class. This group of office workers, technicians, shopkeepers, and craftsmen live in modest but comfortable homes or apartments. Education and communication, government and industry are creating new opportunities for these people today.

Contrasts in housing can be seen in Abu Dhabi, capital city of the United Emirates. Oil development has brought prosperity to Abu Dhabi and few, if any, of the natives of the city could be called poor. The shacks in the foreground are probably housing for newcomers from undeveloped Arab countries who have come to Abu Dhabi for work on new construction or in the oil industry. Beyond are middle-class apartments and commercial office buildings.

Here in this business district of Algiers, modern buildings intermingle with traditional Arab architecture. The rectangular-shaped minaret of the mosque in the background is typical of those found in North Africa.

In the booming cities of the oil-rich nations, traffic is a problem because of the old narrow streets. Much of the old downtown Jeddah had to be torn down to make way for this new business section where automobiles can be parked. Modern office buildings have replaced the trading houses of earlier times.

The sun shines daily in most of the Arab countries and the people spend much of their free time outdoors. From my balcony in Cairo I used to watch a young student studying his lessons on the flat roof of the house next door while his younger brothers and sisters played in the small courtyard adjoining. The maid servant washed the clothes in the same courtyard and hung them to dry on the rooftop. The streets are always teeming with people, even when shops are closed. In the evening it is cool, and pleasant to stroll up and down or simply sit at street cafes. Except in very sophisticated cities like Beirut, it is only men who visit the cafes.

In the past, women in Arab cities did not work, but remained secluded in their homes. They were kept busy raising their families, keeping house, and occasionally visiting friends. But this too is changing. Women now work as clerks in offices and shops, as scientists in research labs, as teachers in the city schools, as doctors, nurses, or technicians in city hospitals, or as newscasters or announcers at radio or TV stations.

But even today most Arab girls do not have the freedom of girls in the West. My young friend, Leila, is eighteen. She works in an office and comes home to lunch every day. In the evening she may join her girlfriends at an open-air cinema or a theatre. Or sometimes she may plan a party with her brother to go swimming or play tennis. But there is no "dating," and certainly no going out alone with young men. Her parents expect to know exactly how she spends her free time — where and how and with whom.

Arabs have a very strong sense of family. There is respect for older people and young people seem far more willing to accept their wisdom and guidance than they do in our Western society. An Arab man has been instilled with a protective feeling for all his family, but especially for his female relatives. This is why it is rare for an Arab girl to be given the freedom that Western girls take for granted.

The traditional Arab family has always been a close-knit unit since the early family tribal times. Grandparents, aunts, uncles, and cousins live and work together, helping each other. When Leila's brother was ill, it was not long before relatives dropped by to inquire about him and offer help. It would be unthinkable for any elderly relative to be left to live alone or sent to an old people's home. Modern living in apartments has tended to separate families, scattering them throughout the city. But there is always some member of the family who has a spare room when one is needed. Three generations live in Leila's home — her parents, her grandmother, and several brothers and sisters.

More and more the bright lights of the city lure young people from the villages and Bedouin tents. They are moving into the major cities in growing numbers to take jobs in factories, shops, and offices. But in spite of the glossy modern conveniences available in a city — the air-conditioning, refrigeration, and television — the change will not be an easy one. For the newcomer with no training and no experience, jobs with good salaries will be scarce. An ambitious young Bedouin or village youth will often have to settle for a low-paying job as an office boy or shopkeeper's assistant. He will probably have to live in a small, drab, rented room in a crowded house with little money to spend on the newly-discovered luxuries.

At the old markets and shops like this one in Cairo, goods are displayed in the street. Such markets are still to be found in cities all over the Arab World. But supermarkets, with their greater variety of goods, are gaining in popularity. They, too, can be found in many Arab cities. But in new cities like Dubai or Abu Dhabi they are used mostly by foreigners.

In a modern jewelry store in Kuwait two men are buying gold ornaments for their wives. The traditionally-dressed women remain modestly in the background and will have no conversation with the clerks. But they will express their wishes quietly to their husbands who will then do the ordering.

As with nomads and villagers, many city families still invest their savings in gold and silver ornaments.

Western and Japanese goods dominate the window display of this applicance store in Kuwait. In the oil-rich countries, the new wealth has created a huge demand for consumer products like these among city workers.

In spite of supermarkets and modern stores, Arab city folk still enjoy doing business at traditional shops where buying and selling are carried on in a leisurely atmosphere over cups of coffee. Customers visiting this yard goods shop in Jeddah may spend an hour or so choosing dress material for their families. Most of the silk cloth on display comes from India. The cotton goods are probably from Egypt.

The stepped-up pace of city living — the noise, the traffic, and the constant coming and going of people — is likely to be confusing and disturbing to the newcomer after the quiet of the desert or the simple rhythm of village life.

If the newcomer manages to adjust to the city and succeeds in getting a better-salaried job, he may decide to marry a girl from his village or tribe. She, too, will find it difficult to adapt to the new life style, for she will miss her family and find the stepped-up pace bewildering.

For those who can afford to live in them, the modern Arab cities offer many attractions. There are theatres, movies, television, and sports. Movies from Europe and America attract large audiences, but the Arabs also have their own film industry and their own favorite film stars. Soccer is very popular and city stadiums are packed with fans when two good teams are playing.

These Jeddah businessmen lunch in a downtown hotel restaurant, Western-style. Other than the traditionally dressed man in the foreground, there is little in this picture that would not be typical of a city hotel restaurant anywhere in the world.

45

City schoolboys in Jeddah put on a tumbling demonstration for their classmates. Education in Arab countries has been greatly influenced by the schools of the West. Physical education is now a basic part of the program in most Arab city schools.

A forest of television antennas blocks the view of a traditional minaret in Kuwait. TV viewing has become as much a part of daily life in Arab cities as it has in the Western world and Japan.

The buildings in the foreground are low-cost houses built for workers by the government.

The camera records a tense moment of action in a city soccer match in Bahrain. Soccer, an import from the West, has spread throughout the Arab World and competition between top teams from the various countries is keen. As in Europe, Arab sports fans know the game as "football."

Walking along the streets of a modern Arab city with its tall office buildings and the never-ceasing flow of traffic, you may think "this could be my home town." But then, above the noise of the traffic, you hear the Call to Prayer from loudspeakers placed around a minaret. Then you become aware that Arab cities have their own rich, age-old culture blending subtly with a modern progressive society.

In the old markets the throngs still swarm about the vendors and the local craftsmen work as they have for centuries. Men and women in traditional robes mingle with those in Western-style dress in downtown streets. The old tribal patterns, separating men and women in leisure hours, still remain. The Arab cities, from North Africa to the Arabian Gulf, still share their common traditions.

ABOUT THE AUTHOR

Doreen Ingrams, British author and traveler, lived for many years in South Arabia, where she traveled widely in previously unknown territory and was awarded, jointly with her husband, the Royal Geographic Society's Gold Medal and the Royal Asian Society's Lawrence of Arabia Medal. She worked for years in the British Broadcasting Corporation's Arabic Service in charge of various programs. At one time or another, she has visited all the countries of the Arab World.

Mrs. Ingrams is the author of three books: *A Survey of Social and Economic Conditions in the Aden Protectorate,* published in 1949; *A Time in Arabia,* published in 1970; and *Palestine Papers 1917–1922: Seeds of Conflict,* published in 1972. She has also written numerous articles and scripts for broadcasting. She is on the Executive Committee of the Council for the Advancement of Arab-British Understanding.

ABOUT THE PRINCIPAL PHOTOGRAPHER

Alistair Duncan was born in India in 1927 and raised in England, his present home. His first contact with the Arab countries was during his service in the British Army. In 1961, h was commissioned to take color photographs in the biblical lands for an edition of the R.S.V. Bible. Other photographic assignments in Arab countries evolved from this, and he decided to give up his career as an insurance broker to become a professional photographer. He also formed the Middle East Archive, an extensive repository of photographs of the Middle East countries as well as other parts of the Arab World. His work has appeared internationally over a wide range of books and publications, including his own picture books, *Land of the Rock* and *The Noble Sanctuary.* He travels widely in the Arab World in the course of his work as a writer and photographer.